THE OPTIONS COURSE
WORKBOOK

WILEY TRADING ADVANTAGE

THE OPTIONS COURSE WORKBOOK

Step-by-step exercises and tests to help you master THE OPTIONS COURSE

George A. Fontanills

JOHN WILEY & SONS, INC.

New York • Chichester • Weinheim • Brisbane • Singapore • Toronto

Copyright © 1998 by George A. Fontanills and Richard Cawood. All rights reserved.

Published by John Wiley & Sons, Inc.

Published simultaneously in Canada.

This publication is designed to provide accurate and authoritative information in regard to the subject matter covered. It is sold with the understanding that the publisher is not engaged in rendering professional services. If professional advice or other expert assistance is required, the services of a competent professional person should be sought.

Library of Congress Cataloging-in-Publication Data:

ISBN 0-471-24949-1

Printed in the United States of America
10 9 8 7 6 5 4 3 2

Contents

Part Two: Answers

PART ONE

Questions

1

Introduction to Options Trading

This introductory chapter explores the reasons why people trade. By offering guidelines for successful trading, it advises the reader on how to develop one's own personal approach to trading and thereby reduce stress and increase confidence.

1. True or False: Just because someone is licensed to place a trade does not necessarily mean that person has the knowledge to invest your money wisely.

2. What is the difference between an investor and a trader?

   _____

   _____

   _____

3. Successful options traders use only _____ that are readily available and can be invested in a sound manner.
   A. Options
   B. Funds
   C. Futures
   D. Stocks

4. When creating a trade (long-term vs. short-term), it is critical to accurately assess your _____ to determine the style of investing that suits you best.
   A. Flexibility
   B. Interest
   C. Markets
   D. Time constraints

5. How can you minimize your losses when you first begin trading options?
   A. Start small
   B. Learn to paper trade
   C. Interview several brokers before picking one
   D. All of the above

6. What is the most important factor of building a low-stress invest-
    ment strategy?
    A. Understanding your markets
    B. Having a good broker
    C. Defining your risk in every trade
    D. Learning to paper trade first

7. _____ allows a trader to cultivate a matrix of strate-
    gies with which to respond to market movement in any direc-
    tion.
    A. Flexibility
    B. Specializing
    C. Computer access
    D. Confidence

8. Successful investors usually _____ in just one or just
    a few areas. This allows them to develop strategies that work in
    certain recognizable market conditions.
    A. Specialize
    B. Win
    C. Go short
    D. Systematically invest

9. To become a successful options trader you have to have
    _____ .

    A. Lots of money to invest
    B. Patience and persistence
    C. A computer
    D. A good sense of market direction

2

The Big Picture

This chapter is designed to give the novice trader an overall view of trading by exploring the fundamentals of stocks, futures, and options. Particular attention is devoted to determining trading instrument properties and describing specific examples.

1. A stock is a unit of ownership in a company. The value of that unit of ownership is based on a number of factors including:

_____

_____

_____

2. Six people form a company together and decide that there will be only six shareholders with only one share each. If this company has assets totaling $90,000 and has $15,000 in liabilities, how much is each share worth?

   A. $15,000
   B. $12,500
   C. $10,000
   D. $7,500

3. The computerized market _____ , is also referred to as the over-the-counter (OTC) market.

   A. Securities and Exchange Commission
   B. Chicago Board Options Exchange
   C. NASDAQ
   D. Wall Street Journal On-line

4. Supply and demand for a company's shares helps to create _____ .

   A. Momentum
   B. Historical volatility
   C. Liquidity
   D. Time decay

5. If investors feel a company will beat the street expectation, then the price of the shares will _____ , as there will be more buyers than sellers.
    A. Be higher
    B. Be lower
    C. Be bid up
    D. Decline

6. If the majority of the investors feel that the company's earnings will disappoint the street, then the prices will _____ .
    A. Be higher
    B. Be lower
    C. Be bid up
    D. Decline

7. If there are more bidders (buyers) prices will _____ .
    If there are more people offering (sellers), prices will _____ .

8. A company's board of directors decides whether to declare a _____ , and whether from time to time it is to be paid out and distributed to shareholders on a payable date.
    A. Better than expected earnings
    B. Revised expected earnings
    C. Cash flow
    D. Dividend

9. What are the three unofficial size classifications of stocks?

    _____

    _____

    _____

10. The _____ , which reports the performance of 30 major companies representing key industries, is the most widely quoted indicator of market performance.

    A. Standard and Poor's Index
    B. AMEX Market Value Index
    C. New York Stock Exchange Composite Index
    D. Dow Jones Industrial Average

11. Name a few stock sectors.

    _____

    _____

    _____

    _____

12. What is the difference between a futures contract and an options contract?

    _____

13. _____ were initially used by farmers and producers of products to hedge themselves or lock in prices for a certain crop or product cycle.

    A. Options contracts
    B. Futures contracts
    C. Stock contracts
    D. All of the above

14. _____ use futures trading to lock in prices and protect themselves from market movement because they are primarily interested in actually receiving or selling the commodities themselves.

    A. Producers
    B. Speculators
    C. Hedgers
    D. Farmers

15. _____ do not expect to take delivery of a product; they are in the futures market to try to make money on the price movement of a futures contract.
    - A. Producers
    - B. Speculators
    - C. Hedgers
    - D. Farmers

16. If you believe soybean prices will rise in the next three months, based on whatever information you may have, you could _____ the soybean futures contract three months out to make a profit.
    - A. Go long
    - B. Go short
    - C. Hedge
    - D. All of the above

17. If you believe corn prices will fall during this same period, you could _____ the corn futures contract three months out to make profit.
    - A. Go long
    - B. Go short
    - C. Hedge
    - D. All of the above

18. _____ commodities are any bulk good traded on an exchange or in the cash market; examples include grains, meats, metals, and energies. _____ commodities include debt instruments (such as bonds), currencies, and indexes.

19. Name a few physical commodity markets.

    _____

    _____

    _____

    _____

20. The value of _____ primarily depends on interest rates.
    A. Bonds
    B. Debt instruments
    C. Eurodollars
    D. All of the above

21. Typically, there is an inverse relationship between _____ and most foreign currencies.
    A. The U.S. dollar
    B. Interest rates
    C. Bonds
    D. All of the above

22. _____ is an indicator that is used to measure and report value changes in a specific group of stocks, commodities, or sectors of the marketplace.
    A. A bond
    B. A moving average
    C. An index
    D. All of the above

23. By combining futures with _____ , you can create trades in which you limit your risk and maximize your potential profits.
    A. Call options
    B. Put options
    C. Futures contracts
    D. All of the above

24. _____ are contracts between two parties that convey to the buyer a right, but not an obligation, to buy or sell a specific commodity or stock at a specific price within a specific time period for a premium.
    A. Stocks
    B. Futures
    C. Options
    D. All of the above

25. The price of an option is referred to as the _____ .
    A. Premium
    B. Strike price
    C. Bid/ask price
    D. P/E: Price to earnings ratio

26. The _____ is referred to as the price at which the stock or commodity underlying a call or put option can be purchased or sold over the specified period.
    A. Premium
    B. Strike price
    C. Bid/ask price
    D. P/E: Price to earnings ratio

27. An option is no longer valid after its _____ .
    A. Payable date
    B. Expiration date
    C. Exercise date
    D. Assignment date

28. True or False: Options are available on all stocks and futures.

29. Each stock option represents _____ shares of a stock.
    A. 50
    B. 100
    C. 500
    D. 1000

30. True or False: Each futures market has a set of unique specifications.

31. An option contract that uses a futures market index (e.g., S&P 500) as the underlying instrument usually values each contract at _____ times the underlying index.
    A. $100
    B. $250
    C. $500
    D. $1000

32. You must be cautious trading indexes, for a few of them do not have much _____ .
    A. Diversification
    B. Liquidity
    C. Cash value
    D. Flexibility

33. The most important factors of determining opportunity in a market are _____ .
    A. Volume and cash flow
    B. Volatility and cash flow
    C. Liquidity and cash flow
    D. Liquidity and volatility

34. _____ gives you the opportunity to move in and out of a market with ease.
    A. Volatility
    B. Flexibility
    C. Inexpensive options
    D. Liquidity

35. _____ measures the amount by which an underlying instrument is expected to fluctuate in a given period of time.
    A. Volatility
    B. Delta
    C. Theta
    D. Liquidity

3

Elements of a Good Investment

This chapter offers guidelines that enhance a trader's ability to make profitable trades. It introduces several concepts including low risk, time requirements, and risk tolerance as well as casting a glance at risk profiles and investment criteria.

1. Name as many elements as you can of a good investment.

    _____

    _____

    _____

    _____

2. _____ of any investment must take into account the
    following elements: potential risk, potential reward, the probability
    of success, and how long the investment takes to make a return.
    A. Limiting the risk
    B. The risk/reward profile
    C. The delta neutrality
    D. All of the above

3. Studying a risk profile can show you the potential increasing or de-
    creasing profit and loss of a trade relative to the underlying asset's
    _____ over a specific period of time.
    A. Volatility
    B. Volume
    C. Price
    D. Change in direction

4. The best investments will have an opportunity for _____
    with acceptable risk and a high probability of winning on a con-
    sistent basis.
    A. High reward
    B. High volatility
    C. High liquidity
    D. Major market movement

5. True or False: If you do not have the time to sit in front of a com-
    puter day in and day out, then your best investments will be day
    trades.

6. Your risk tolerance level is directly proportional to your
    _____ .
    A. Knowledge of the markets
    B. Computer availability
    C. Time requirements
    D. Available investment capital

7. Name a few investment criteria other than simply making money.

    _____

    _____

    _____

4

A Short Course in Investment Economics

This chapter explores the economic interrelationships among interest rates, bond prices, and stocks. These typical relationships provide a stable foundation from which traders can make consistent profits.

1. The _____ has a corresponding futures contract that is traded at the Chicago Board of Trade and reflects an important aspect of many people's lives, mortgage interest rates.

    A. S&P 500

    B. OEX

    C. 10-year notes

    D. 30-year T-bond

2. In a typical situation, if interest rates go up, bond prices go _____ .

    A. Up

    B. Down

    C. Stay the same

    D. You can never really tell

3. Bond prices and the stock market should _____ .

    A. Go in the same direction

    B. Have an inverse relationship

    C. Go in opposite directions

    D. Have no relationship whatsoever

4. If interest rates go sideways, stock prices will probably _____ .

    A. Rise

    B. Fall

    C. Go sideways

    D. Rise at first and then fall steadily

5. There are periods when _____ occurs and a stock's earnings increase regardless of whether interest rates go up or down.

    A. An inverse relationship

    B. A contrarian effect

    C. A divergence

    D. A momentum push

6. If you see interest rates _____ quickly, you don't want to be a buyer of stocks.

    A. Increasing

    B. Decreasing

    C. Increasing sharply and then falling off

    D. Decreasing slowly and then rising

7. If you find that interest rates are _____ , being a buyer of stocks is a good idea, because the stock market has an upward bias.

    A. Increasing

    B. Decreasing

    C. Stable or increasing

    D. Stable or decreasing

5

How to Spot Explosive Opportunities

In this chapter, the reader is introduced to a wide variety of methods that can be used to locate profitable trading opportunities. The formal techniques of fundamental and technical analysis are reviewed as well as various media sources, including the *Wall Street Journal*, *Investor's Business Daily*, and CNBC. In addition, a few informal techniques—from using the contrarian approach to critiquing products you own—are recommended. A few effective stock indicators are also explored.

1. The two general forms of market analysis are _____
   and _____ .

2. _____ analysis is primarily concerned with the un-
   derlying factors of supply and demand for a stock or commodity.
   A. Fundamental
   B. Technical

3. Name three factors of fundamental analysis.

   _____

   _____

   _____

4. _____ analysis is primarily concerned with statistics
   generated by market activity and the resulting price patterns and
   trends.
   A. Fundamental
   B. Technical

5. Name two techniques of technical analysis.

   _____

   _____

6. A _____ , probably the simplest and most widely
   used technical tool, calculates price action over a specified period
   of time on a median basis.
   A. Technical chart
   B. Moving average
   C. Momentum indicator
   D. Contrarian approach

7. A _____ utilizes price and volume statistics for predicting the strength or weakness of a current market and any overbought or oversold conditions.

   A. Technical chart

   B. Moving average

   C. Momentum indicator

   D. Contrarian approach

8. If you use the _____ approach, you will be trading against the majority view of the marketplace.

   A. Charting

   B. Moving averages

   C. Momentum indicators

   D. Contrarian

9. True or False: Fundamental analysis and technical analysis are mutually exclusive—traders should learn to use one or the other.

10. By studying the daily reactions of specific markets to _____ , you can begin to forecast which strategy can be used to make the largest potential profit.

   A. Interest rates

   B. Seasonal changes

   C. Government reports

   D. All of the above

11. While shopping in a retail store, name three ways you can spot potentially profitable investments.

_____

_____

_____

12. Name four ways to spot potential investments in your everyday life.

    _____

    _____

    _____

    _____

13. List three ways data service providers can relay information.

    _____

    _____

    _____

14. True or False: If you are going to sit in front of a computer all day long, you don't really need real-time quotes.

15. _____ was born from the Financial News Network (FNN), which was watched widely by the investment community.

    A. CNN Business
    B. CNBC
    C. CBS
    D. Fox

16. The best investments will have _____ , which should be monitored over both a short and long period of time.

    A. Cheap options
    B. Low margin
    C. Momentum
    D. Low volatility

17. An increase in a stock's _____ signals movement and a good opportunity for investment.
    A. Price
    B. Volume
    C. Perceived risk
    D. All of the above

18. The best investments will have a reasonable _____ compared to the industry average.
    A. Settle
    B. Yield and percent
    C. P/E
    D. Open interest

19. Name six ways to spot potential profit-making stock opportunities.

    _____

    _____

    _____

    _____

    _____

    _____

20. Who seems to have a golden touch when it comes to building megabuck corporations?

    _____

21. A low-priced stock trades for less than _____ .
    A. $10
    B. $20
    C. $30
    D. $50

22. Why is it easier to make money on low-priced stocks?

    A. You can make a high return faster

    B. You have less invested to lose

    C. You can play more stocks with less money

    D. All of the above

23. The theory behind _____ , the basis of a mutual fund, is that a larger group of stocks will even out the chances of winning in the long run.

    A. A diversification

    B. Broad portfolio

    C. Both A and B

    D. Neither A nor B

24. Momentum investors are much more _____-oriented than mutual fund investors or money managers.

    A. Short-term

    B. Long-term

    C. Volatility

    D. Profit

25. A long-term indicator of momentum can be measured by looking for a change in the price of a stock over the previous _____ .

    A. 15 days

    B. 30 days

    C. 60 days

    D. 90 days

    E. Both A and B

    F. Both C and D

26. If a stock has increased or decreased in price more than _____ since yesterday, this can be used to indicate a momentum investment.
    A. 5 percent
    B. 10 percent
    C. 15 percent
    D. 30 percent

27. In order to get a better understanding of a stock's profitability, take a look at its _____ .
    A. Price and volume
    B. Volatility
    C. Liquidity
    D. Range

28. If a stock trades less than _____ shares daily, avoid it.
    A. 100,000
    B. 300,000
    C. 500,000
    D. 1,000,000

29. To apply the contrarian approach, look at the _____ list to find stocks that have made major moves down (50 percent or greater) and then look for a rebound.
    A. Price percentage gainers
    B. Price percentage losers
    C. Volume percentage leaders
    D. Lifetime high and low

30. The blow-off bottom may have occurred when a stock has made and is coming off a new _____ .
    A. High price
    B. High volume
    C. Low price
    D. Low volume

6

Option Basics

This chapter gives an in-depth analysis of call and put options. Particular attention is paid to strike prices, premiums, expiration dates, and recognizing whether an option is in-the-money, at-the-money, or out-of-the-money. The reader is also introduced to which basic option strategies are most appropriate in bullish and bearish markets.

1. _____ gives the buyer the right, but not the obligation, to buy or sell a specified number of shares or contracts of the
   underlying security or derivative at a predetermined price during a
   set period of time.

   A. A futures contract

   B. An option

   C. A stock

   D. A derivative

2. If you sign a 12-month lease agreement with an option to buy a
   house at $200,000 and the seller charges $1000 extra just for that
   12-month option to buy the house, that charge is called the option
   _____ .

   A. Strike price

   B. Expiration

   C. Credit

   D. Premium

3. True or False: Options are available on all futures and stocks.

4. True or False: Once you own an option, you are obligated to buy
   or sell the underlying instrument.

5. Once an option _____ , you lose your right to buy or
   sell the underlying instrument at the specified price.

   A. Moves in-the-money

   B. Moves out-of-the-money

   C. Expires

   D. None of the above

6. Options, when bought, are done so at a _____ to the
   buyer.

   A. Debit

   B. Credit

   C. Margin

   D. All of the above

7. Options, when sold, are done so by giving a _____ to the seller.
   A. Debit
   B. Credit
   C. Margin
   D. All of the above

8. Options are available at several _____ representing the price of the underlying instrument.
   A. Premiums
   B. Margins
   C. Expiration dates
   D. Strike prices

9. The more time until expiration, the more _____ the premium.
   A. Expensive
   B. Inexpensive

10. True or False: Strike prices for stocks usually come in multiples of five.

11. Name the three possible relationships strike prices have to the current price of the underlying security.

   _____

   _____

   _____

12. What is the difference between American style options and European style options?

   _____

   _____

13. What are the three possible resolutions of an option contract?

_____

_____

_____

14. If the writer of an option receives _____ , the option has been assigned and the writer is obligated to buy or sell the specified amount of underlying assets at the strike price to the holder.

    A. A margin call

    B. An assignment notice

    C. An exercise notice

    D. None of the above

15. A stock option represents the right to buy or sell _____ shares of the underlying stock.

    A. 50

    B. 100

    C. 250

    D. 500

16. The expiration date is typically the _____ Friday of the expiration month for stock options.

    A. First

    B. Second

    C. Third

    D. Last

17. Strike prices for stock options come in increments of _____ for other than lower-priced stocks.

    A. $1

    B. $2

    C. $5

    D. $10

18. True or False: The strike price and expiration date of futures options differ depending on the underlying instrument they represent.

19. Name the two types of options.

_____

_____

20. _____ gives the buyer the right (not the obligation) to buy the underlying futures or stock contract.
    A. A call option
    B. A put option
    C. A futures option contract
    D. A stock option contract

21. If the market price is more than your strike price, your call option is _____ .
    A. At-the-money
    B. In-the-money
    C. Out-of-the-money

22. If the market price is less than your strike price, your call option is _____ .
    A. At-the-money
    B. In-the-money
    C. Out-of-the-money

23. If the market price is the same as your strike price, your option is _____ .
    A. At-the-money
    B. In-the-money
    C. Out-of-the-money

24. If you buy call options, you are _____ the market.
    A. Going long
    B. Going short
    C. Going delta neutral
    D. Hedging

25. If you sell call options, you are _____ the market.
    A. Going long
    B. Going short
    C. Going delta neutral
    D. Hedging

26. If you are _____ (you believe the market will rise), then you want to buy calls.
    A. Bearish
    B. Bullish

27. If you are _____ (you believe the market will drop), then you want to sell calls.
    A. Bearish
    B. Bullish

28. If you buy a call option, your risk is _____ .
    A. Unlimited
    B. The price of the underlying asset
    C. The margin of the underlying asset
    D. The price of the premium and brokerage commissions

29. If you sell a call option, your risk is _____ .
    A. Unlimited
    B. The price of the underlying asset
    C. The margin of the underlying asset
    D. The price of the premium

30. If the current price of the underlying asset is 300, fill in the call option blanks (ITM, ATM, or OTM).

Strike Price of Option	Call Option
320	_____
315	_____
310	_____
305	_____
300	_____
295	_____
290	_____
285	_____
280	_____

31. Name the two ways profits can be realized from purchasing a call option.

_____

_____

32. All the options of one type (put or call) that have the same underlying security, expiration date, and strike price are called _____ .
    A. An option class
    B. An option series
    C. An option division
    D. An option suit

33. _____ gives the buyer the right (not the obligation) to sell the underlying futures or stock contract.
    A. A call option
    B. A put option
    C. A futures option contract
    D. A stock option contract

34. If the market price is less than your strike price, your put option is
    _____ .
    A. At-the-money
    B. In-the-money
    C. Out-of-the-money

35. If the market price is more than your strike price, your put option is
    _____ .
    A. At-the-money
    B. In-the-money
    C. Out-of-the-money

36. If the market price is the same as your strike price, your put option
    is _____ .
    A. At-the-money
    B. In-the-money
    C. Out-of-the-money

37. If you buy put options, you are _____ the market.
    A. Going long
    B. Going short
    C. Going delta neutral
    D. Hedging

38. If you sell put options, you are _____ the market.
    A. Going long
    B. Going short
    C. Going delta neutral
    D. Hedging

39. If the market is _____ , then you want to buy puts.
    A. Bearish
    B. Bullish

40. If the market is _____ , then you want to sell puts.
    A. Bearish
    B. Bullish

41. If you buy a put option, your risk is _____ .
    A. Unlimited
    B. The price of the underlying asset
    C. The margin of the underlying asset
    D. The price of the premium and brokerage commissions

42. If you sell a put option, your risk is _____ .
    A. Unlimited
    B. The price of the underlying asset
    C. The margin of the underlying asset
    D. The price of the premium

43. If the current price of the underlying asset is 300, fill in the put option blanks (ITM, ATM, or OTM).

Strike Price of Option	Put Option
320	_____
315	_____
310	_____
305	_____
300	_____
295	_____
290	_____
285	_____
280	_____

7

Introduction to Delta Neutral Trading

In this chapter, the reader is introduced to the basics of delta neutral trading. Two of the most important market characteristics—volatility and liquidity—are discussed at length. In addition, a Greek options term, the delta, is studied in detail and the initial technique of delta neutral trading explored.

1. Locating opportunities for delta neutral trades depends on finding markets with _____ .
   A. High liquidity and high volatility
   B. High liquidity and low volatility
   C. Low liquidity and high volatility
   D. Low liquidity and low volatility
   E. Both A & B
   F. Both C & D

2. True or False: The higher an asset's volatility, the higher the price of its options.

3. A market's _____ can be defined as the volume of trading activity that enables a trader to buy or sell a security or derivative and receive fair value for it.
   A. Volatility
   B. Equilibrium level
   C. Support
   D. Liquidity

4. True or False: Delta neutral strategies are suitable for day trading.

5. An option's delta can be roughly calculated by _____ .
   A. Dividing the change in the premium by the change in the price of the underlying asset
   B. Dividing the change in the price of the underlying asset by the change in the premium
   C. Multiplying the change in the premium by the change in the price of the underlying asset
   D. Multiplying the change in the price of the underlying asset by the change in the premium

6. Futures have fixed deltas of _____ .
   A. Plus 50
   B. Minus 50
   C. Plus or minus 50
   D. Plus or minus 100

7. Long call options have _____ deltas.
   A. Positive
   B. Negative

8. Short put options have _____ deltas.
   A. Positive
   B. Negative

9. As a rule of thumb, the deeper _____ your option is, the higher the delta.
   A. In-the-money
   B. Out-of-the-money

10. _____ options have a delta of plus or minus 50.
    A. In-the-money
    B. Out-of-the-money
    C. At-the-money

11. When an option is very deep _____ , it will start acting very much like a futures contract.
    A. In-the-money
    B. Out-of-the-money

12. Two long Treasury bond futures contracts have a delta of
    _____ .

    A. Minus 100
    B. Minus 200
    C. Plus 100
    D. Plus 200

8

The Greeks and Option Pricing

The option Greeks are a set of measurements that provide insight into a trade's risk exposure. This chapter reviews the five basic option Greeks and analyzes their trading applications. In addition, the reader examines how intrinsic value, time value, and volatility impact option premiums.

1. Option Greeks are a set of measurements that explore the
   _____ of a specific trade.
   A. Parameters
   B. Delta neutral opportunities
   C. Risk exposures
   D. Risk-to-reward ratios

2. Name five option Greeks.

   _____

   _____

   _____

   _____

   _____

3. Fill in the option Greek term next to its appropriate definition.

Greek	*Definition*
_____	Change in the delta of an option with respect to the change in price of its underlying security
_____	The percentage change in an option's price per 1 percent change in implied volatility
_____	Change in the price of an option relative to the price change of the underlying security
_____	Change in the price of an option with respect to a change in its time to expiration
_____	Change in the price of an option with respect to its change in volatility

4. The two most important components of an option's premium are
   _____ and _____ .
   A. Intrinsic value and extrinsic value
   B. Vega and extrinsic value
   C. Intrinsic value and vega
   D. Zeta and theta

5. Intrinsic value is defined as the amount by which the strike price of an option is _____ .

   A. At-the-money

   B. In-the-money

   C. Out-of-the-money

6. For a call option, intrinsic value is equal to _____ .

   A. The strike price of the call option minus the current price of the underlying asset

   B. The strike price of the call option plus the current price of the underlying asset

   C. The current price of the underlying asset minus the strike price of the call option

   D. The current price of the underlying asset plus the strike price of the call option

7. For a put option, intrinsic value is equal to _____ .

   A. The strike price of the put option minus the current price of the underlying asset

   B. The strike price of the put option plus the current price of the underlying asset

   C. The current price of the underlying asset minus the strike price of the put option

   D. The current price of the underlying asset plus the strike price of the put option

8. If a call or put option is at-the-money, the intrinsic value is equal to _____ .

   A. The strike price of the option

   B. The price of the underlying asset

   C. The price of the underlying asset minus the strike price of the option

   D. Zero

9. If a call or put option is out-of-the-money, the intrinsic value is equal to _____ .

   A. The strike price of the option
   B. The price of the underlying asset
   C. The price of the underlying asset minus the strike price of the option
   D. Zero

10. True or False: The intrinsic value of an option does not depend on how much time is left until expiration.

11. Time value _____ as an option approaches expiration.

    A. Increases
    B. Decreases
    C. Stays the same

12. Time value is also known as _____ .

    A. Delta
    B. Gamma
    C. Theta
    D. Vega
    E. Zeta

13. _____ can be defined as the amount by which the price of an option exceeds its intrinsic value.

    A. Extrinsic value
    B. Time value
    C. Theta
    D. All of the above

14. Complete the gold table below where the current price is 300.

Price of Gold = 300

Call Strike Price	January	March	Intrinsic Value	Time Value Jan	Time Value Mar
295	12.5	15.75			
300	5	8.5			
305	1.5	3.75			

15. The more _____ an option is, the less it costs.
    A. At-the-money
    B. In-the-money
    C. Out-of-the-money

16. On expiration day, an option's worth is its _____ .
    A. Time value
    B. Extrinsic value
    C. Intrinsic value
    D. Fair market value

17. The deeper _____ a call or put option is, the more the option moves more like the underlying asset.
    A. In-the-money
    B. Out-of-the-money

18. Name the seven components that contribute to option pricing.

    _____

    _____

    _____

    _____

    _____

    _____

    _____

19. _____ is defined as a measurement of the amount by which an underlying asset is expected to fluctuate in a given period of time.

   A. Rate-free interest rate

   B. Liquidity

   C. Dividend payment

   D. Volatility

20. Name and describe the two kinds of volatility.

   _____

   _____

   _____

   _____

21. Name three things understanding volatility can help you to accomplish.

   _____

   _____

   _____

22. _____ is the term that represents volatility.

   A. Delta

   B. Gamma

   C. Theta

   D. Vega

   E. Zeta

23. As the option moves quicker within time, volatility moves _____ .

   A. Up

   B. Down

   C. Sideways

24. The release of the employment report on the _____
of each month stimulates a rise in volatility in the bond market.
    A. First Monday
    B. First Friday
    C. Second Monday
    D. Third Friday

25. Buying options when the implied volatility _____
can cause some trades to end up losing even when the price of the
underlying asset moves in your direction.
    A. Rises
    B. Drops
    C. Stays the same for more than one week
    D. Stays the same for more than one month

26. When an option's actual price differs from the theoretical price by
any significant amount, you can take advantage of the situation by
_____ expecting the prices to fall back in line as the
expiration date approaches.
    A. Selling options with low volatility and buying options with high
       volatility
    B. Selling or buying options with low volatility
    C. Buying options with low volatility and selling options with high
       volatility
    D. Buying or selling options with high volatility

9
Risk Profiles

A risk profile is a graphical representation of the overall risk of a specific trade. By visualizing the potential risk and reward, a trader is better equipped to find profitable trades. The following six risk graphs are examined in this chapter: long futures, short futures, long call, short call, long put, and short put. More advanced trading strategies are combinations of these basic risk curves.

1. Every trade you place has a corresponding _____
    that graphically shows your potential risk and potential reward
    over a range of prices and time.

    A. Risk curve

    B. Risk graph

    C. Risk profile

    D. All of the above

2. The horizontal numbers at the bottom of a risk profile chart show
    the _____ .

    A. Market price of the underlying asset

    B. Option premium price

    C. Profit and loss

    D. Change in overall position delta

3. The vertical numbers at the left of a risk profile chart show
    _____ .

    A. Market price of the underlying asset

    B. Option premium price

    C. Profit and loss

    D. Change in overall position delta

4. Label the risk graphs with the correct strategy—long futures (or
    stocks), long call, long put, short futures (or stocks), short call, or
    short put.

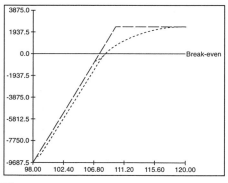

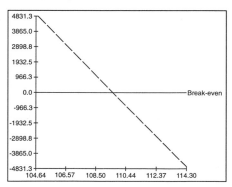

Figure 1 _____   **Figure 2** _____

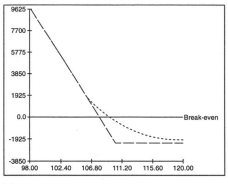

Figure 3 _____

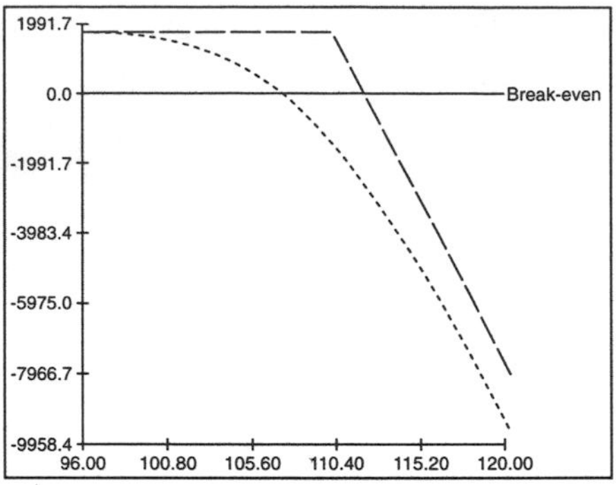

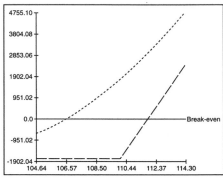

Figure 4 _____

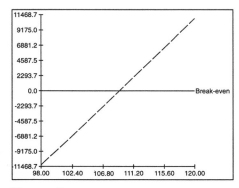

Figure 5 _____

Figure 6 _____

5. The long futures strategy provides _____ .
    A. Limited profit potential with limited risk
    B. Limited profit potential with unlimited risk
    C. Unlimited profit potential with unlimited risk
    D. Unlimited profit potential with limited risk

6. A futures contract does not have premium or time decay; it has a _____ movement in price versus risk and reward.
    A. 1 to 1
    B. 1 to 2
    C. 1 to 10
    D. 1 to 100

7. True or False: In a short futures strategy, when the futures price falls, you make money; when it rises, you lose money.

8. A short futures strategy has virtually _____ .
   A. Limited profit potential with limited risk
   B. Limited profit potential with unlimited risk
   C. Unlimited profit potential with unlimited risk
   D. Unlimited profit potential with limited risk

9. True or False: With a long call strategy, when the price of the underlying asset rises you make money; when it falls, you lose money.

10. A long call strategy has virtually _____ .
    A. Limited profit potential with limited risk
    B. Limited profit potential with unlimited risk
    C. Unlimited profit potential with unlimited risk
    D. Unlimited profit potential with limited risk

11. True or False: With a long call strategy, you have to hold margin in your account to place the trade.

12. If you bought a Sep IBM 105 Call @ 5, your minimum risk on this trade would be _____ .
    A. $50 plus commissions
    B. $100 plus commissions
    C. $500 plus commissions
    D. $1000 plus commissions

13. The break-even of a long call option by expiration is derived by _____ .
    A. Adding the cost of the option to its strike price
    B. Adding cost of the option to the price of the commission
    C. Subtracting the strike price from the option premium
    D. Subtracting the option premium from the strike price

14. True or False: With a short call strategy, when the underlying instrument's price rises, you make money; when it falls, you lose money.

15. A short call strategy has virtually _____ .
    A. Limited profit potential with limited risk
    B. Limited profit potential with unlimited risk
    C. Unlimited profit potential with unlimited risk
    D. Unlimited profit potential with limited risk

16. True or False: With a long put strategy, when the underlying instrument's price falls, you make money; when it rises, you lose money.

17. A long put strategy has _____ .
    A. Limited profit potential with limited risk
    B. Limited profit potential with unlimited risk
    C. Unlimited profit potential with unlimited risk
    D. Unlimited profit potential with limited risk

18. The break-even of a put option by expiration is derived by _____ .
    A. Adding the cost of the option to its strike price
    B. Adding cost of the option to the price of the commission
    C. Subtracting the strike price from the option premium
    D. Subtracting the option premium from the strike price

19. True or False: In a short put strategy, when the underlying instrument's price falls, you make money; when it rises, you lose money.

20. A short put strategy has _____ .
    A. Limited profit potential with limited risk
    B. Limited profit potential with unlimited risk
    C. Unlimited profit potential with unlimited risk
    D. Unlimited profit potential with limited risk

10

Risk and Margin

In this chapter, the basic concepts of risk and margin are explored. Risk is inherent in every trade and is the most important characteristic to a trade's viability. Margin is the amount of cash required to be on deposit with a trader's clearing firm in order to execute a trade. A list of recent margin levels can be found in the Appendixes.

1. What are the two key elements of profitable trades?

    _____

    _____

2. What are the two most important factors in determining the cost of an investment?

    _____

    _____

3. A(n) _____ requires you to put up 100 percent of the money to execute the trade.
    A. Margin trade
    B. Cash trade
    C. Open trade
    D. None of the above

4. A(n) _____ allows you to put up a percentage of the calculated amount in cash, and the rest is on account.
    A. Margin trade
    B. Cash trade
    C. Open trade
    D. None of the above

5. _____ is defined as the amount of cash required to be on deposit with your clearing firm to secure the integrity of the trade.
    A. Deposit
    B. Commission
    C. Adjustment
    D. Margin

6. A _____ allows traders and investors to leverage their assets to produce a higher return.

   A. Cash account

   B. Margin account

   C. Absorption account

   D. Adjunct account

7. Margin accounts allow a trader to extract up to _____ of the cash value of their stock.

   A. 25 percent

   B. 50 percent

   C. 75 percent

   D. 100 percent

8. Using a margin account, if you buy 500 shares of IBM at 100, how much will this trade cost you, not including commissions?

   A. $10,000

   B. $20,000

   C. $25,000

   D. $50,000

9. A _____ from your broker requires you to place additional funds in your account. If you do not place these additional funds in your account, your positions will be liquidated.

   A. Margin ratio

   B. Margin account

   C. Margin requirement

   D. Margin call

10. True or False: If you are trading delta neutral using futures and options, your margin will be close to zero, which means you will never get a margin call.

11. If the _____ of your trade increases, then the margin will also increase.
    A. Implied risk
    B. Risk premium
    C. Risk arbitrage
    D. Perceived risk

12. If you do not have additional funds to place in your account to cover a margin call, your position will be _____ .
    A. Placed on hold
    B. Liquidated
    C. Traded by the brokerage firm
    D. None of the above

13. Based on the rules of the Securities and Exchange Commission and the clearing firms, margin for stocks equals _____ of the amount of the trade.
    A. 25 percent
    B. 35 percent
    C. 50 percent
    D. 75 percent

14. For stock options, each point equals _____ .
    A. $10
    B. $100
    C. $500
    D. Various amounts depending on the stock

15. Selling _____ options or placing an unprotected trade has the highest risk and the highest margin requirements.
    A. Naked
    B. Call
    C. Put
    D. Covered

16. Combining the buying and selling of options, stocks, and/or futures creates a more complex calculation; however, this will _____ your margin requirements.

    A. Increase
    B. Decrease
    C. Not affect
    D. All of the above

17. The margin for _____ varies significantly from market to market due to the volatility of the markets as well as the current price.

    A. Stocks
    B. Options
    C. Commodities
    D. None of the above

18. _____ is the ability to use less capital for a larger potential return but can result in increased risk.

    A. Volatility
    B. Liquidity
    C. Flexibility
    D. Leverage

11

Basic Trading Strategies

In this chapter, the reader delves into the complex world of option strategies. The following six strategies are examined in depth: covered call, covered put, bull call, bull put, bear call, and bear put. An example of each strategy is included to enable the reader to witness a hands-on illustration of each specific trading technique.

1. Name the three fundamental trading approaches.

    _____

    _____

    _____

2. True or False: Strategic trades are typically short-term trading op-
    portunities geared especially for day traders and short-term traders
    who do not have the opportunity to monitor the markets very
    closely each day.

3. True or False: Long-term trades take a while to blossom and bear
    fruit, which gives the long-term trader more time to develop the art
    of patience.

4. Delta neutral trades are hedged when the total position delta
    equals _____ .
    A. +100
    B. –100
    C. +50
    D. –50
    E. Zero

5. Adjustments are made by _____ in such a way to
    bring the overall trade back to delta neutral.
    A. Buying trading instruments
    B. Selling trading instruments
    C. Buying or selling trading instruments
    D. Exiting the trade

6. In a _____ strategy, a trader offsets the existing purchase of a long futures or stock position with the sale of an option.
   A. Covered write
   B. Bear call spread
   C. Bear put spread
   D. Bull call spread
   E. Bull put spread

7. A covered write provides some protection in the price of the underlying asset and is usually used when you do not expect the underlying to _____ sharply in price.
   A. Increase
   B. Decrease
   C. Increase or decrease

8. A covered call strategy has _____ .
   A. Limited profit potential with limited risk
   B. Limited profit potential with unlimited risk
   C. Unlimited profit potential with unlimited risk
   D. Unlimited profit potential with limited risk

9. The _____ is a high-leverage strategy consisting of going long one call at a lower strike price and short one call at a higher strike price.
   A. Covered write
   B. Bear call spread
   C. Bear put spread
   D. Bull call spread
   E. Bull put spread

10. The bull call spread has _____ .
    A. Limited profit potential with limited risk
    B. Limited profit potential with unlimited risk
    C. Unlimited profit potential with unlimited risk
    D. Unlimited profit potential with limited risk

11. Calculate the maximum risk and reward and the break-even for the following bull call spread trade:

> Long 1 Dec Gold Futures 310 Call @ 7.80
> Short 1 Dec Gold Futures 330 Call @ 4.25

Maximum risk =_____

Maximum reward = _____

Break-even = _____

12. In a _____ , you buy the lower-strike put and sell the higher-strike put using the same number of options.
    A. Covered write
    B. Bear call spread
    C. Bear put spread
    D. Bull call spread
    E. Bull put spread

13. A bull put spread has a _____ .
    A. Limited profit potential with limited risk
    B. Limited profit potential with unlimited risk
    C. Unlimited profit potential with unlimited risk
    D. Unlimited profit potential with limited risk

14. Calculate the maximum risk and reward and the break-even for the following bull put spread trade:

> Long 1 Jun Gold Futures 320 Put @ 6.75
> Short 1 Jun Gold Futures 330 Put @ 10.50

Maximum risk = _____

Maximum reward = _____

Break-even = _____

15. In a _____ , you sell the lower-strike call and buy the higher-strike call using the same number of options.

   A. Covered write

   B. Bear call spread

   C. Bear put spread

   D. Bull call spread

   E. Bull put spread

16. A bear call spread has a _____ .

   A. Limited profit potential with limited risk

   B. Limited profit potential with unlimited risk

   C. Unlimited profit potential with unlimited risk

   D. Unlimited profit potential with limited risk

17. Calculate the maximum risk and reward and the break-even for the following bear call spread trade:

   Long 1 Dec IBM 90 Call @ 7.00
   Short 1 Dec IBM 80 Call @ 11.50

   Maximum risk = _____

   Maximum reward = _____

   Break-even = _____

18. In a _____ , you buy a higher-strike price put and sell a lower-strike price put.

   A. Covered write

   B. Bear call spread

   C. Bear put spread

   D. Bull call spread

   E. Bull put spread

19. A bear put spread has a _____ .
    A. Limited profit potential with limited risk
    B. Limited profit potential with unlimited risk
    C. Unlimited profit potential with unlimited risk
    D. Unlimited profit potential with limited risk

20. Calculate the maximum risk and reward for the following bear put spread trade:

    Long 1 Oct Intel 95 Put @ $3\frac{3}{4}$
    Short 1 Oct Intel 90 Put @ $2\frac{1}{2}$

    Maximum risk = _____

    Maximum reward = _____

    Break-even = _____

12

The Nuts and Bolts
of Delta Neutral Trading

This chapter explores several delta neutral strategies, including straddles, strangles, and synthetic straddles. These strategies are based on optimal mathematical relationships and have a high probability of profitability when applied to suitable markets. Examples of each strategy are included to enable the reader to become fully acquainted with the calculations of risk, reward, and break-even.

1. Setting up a delta neutral trade requires selecting a calculated ratio of short and long positions that creates an overall position delta of _____ .

   A. +100
   B. –100
   C. +50
   D. Zero

2. The delta of one futures contract or 100 shares of stock equals plus or minus _____ .

   A. 500
   B. 100
   C. 50
   D. Zero

3. True or False: One hundred shares of any stock or one futures contract equals plus or minus 1000 deltas.

4. The delta of an option depends on its _____ .

   A. Expiration date
   B. Volatility
   C. Strike price
   D. Premium

5. Buying calls is a _____ move.

   A. Bearish
   B. Bullish

6. Buying puts is a _____ move.

   A. Bearish
   B. Bullish

7. Two ways of creating a delta neutral trade with ATM options if you are buying one futures contract would be to also _____ or _____ .

8. Name two ways of creating a delta neutral trade with ATM options if you are selling one futures contract.

_____

_____

9. By purchasing futures and buying puts, a U-shaped risk graph is created that reflects _____ .

A. Limited profit potential with limited risk

B. Limited profit potential with unlimited risk

C. Unlimited profit potential with unlimited risk

D. Unlimited profit potential with limited risk

10. By buying futures and selling calls, an upside-down U-shaped risk graph is created that reflects _____ .

A. Limited profit potential with limited risk

B. Limited profit potential with unlimited risk

C. Unlimited profit potential with unlimited risk

D. Unlimited profit potential with limited risk

11. By selling one S&P 500 futures contract and buying two ATM calls, what kind of risk curve are you creating?

A. U-shaped risk curve with unlimited profit potential and limited risk

B. U-shaped risk curve with limited profit potential and unlimited risk

C. Upside-down U-shaped risk curve with unlimited profit potential and limited risk

D. Upside-down U-shaped risk curve with limited profit potential and unlimited risk

12. By selling one S&P 500 futures contract and selling two ATM puts, what kind of risk curve are you creating?
    A. U-shaped risk curve with unlimited profit potential and limited risk
    B. U-shaped risk curve with limited profit potential and unlimited risk
    C. Upside-down U-shaped risk curve with unlimited profit potential and limited risk
    D. Upside-down U-shaped risk curve with limited profit potential and unlimited risk

13. Buying a straddle involves buying both a call and a put with
    _____ .
    A. Different strike prices and identical expiration months
    B. Identical strike prices and different expiration months
    C. Identical strike prices and expiration months
    D. Different strike prices and expiration months

14. To place a long straddle, it is optimal to locate a market with
    _____ .
    A. High volatility expecting a volatility decrease
    B. Low volatility expecting a volatility increase
    C. Continuous high liquidity
    D. Continuous low liquidity

15. Long straddles create what kind of risk profiles?
    A. U-shaped risk curves with unlimited profit potential and limited risk
    B. U-shaped risk curves with limited profit potential and unlimited risk
    C. Upside-down U-shaped risk curves with unlimited profit potential and limited risk
    D. Upside-down U-shaped risk curves with limited profit potential and unlimited risk

16. How is the upside break-even of a long straddle calculated?

_____

17. How is the downside break-even of a long straddle calculated?

_____

18. Calculate the following values for this long straddle:

> Long 1 Oct ATM Gold Futures 330 Call @ 7.20
> Long 1 Oct ATM Gold Futures 330 Put @ 5.55

Put cost = _____

Call cost = _____

Maximum reward = _____

Maximum risk = _____

Upside break-even = _____

Downside break-even = _____

Range of profitability = _____

19. Selling a straddle involves selling both a call and a put with
    _____ .

    A. Different strike prices and identical expiration months
    B. Identical strike prices and different expiration months
    C. Identical strike prices and expiration months
    D. Different strike prices and expiration months

20. To place a short straddle, you should locate a market with
    _____ .

    A. High volatility
    B. Low volatility
    C. High liquidity
    D. Low liquidity

21. Short straddles create what kind of risk profiles?
    A. U-shaped risk curves with unlimited profit potential and limited risk
    B. U-shaped risk curves with limited profit potential and unlimited risk
    C. Upside-down U-shaped risk curves with unlimited profit potential and limited risk
    D. Upside-down U-shaped risk curves with limited profit potential and unlimited risk

22. Calculate the following values using this short straddle:

    Short 1 Mar Japanese Yen ATM 84 Put @ 2.22
    Short 1 Mar Japanese Yen ATM 84 Call @ 3.24

    Maximum put profit = _____

    Maximum call profit = _____

    Maximum reward = _____

    Maximum risk = _____

    Upside break-even = _____

    Downside break-even = _____

    Range of profitability = _____

23. If the futures in the previous trade move to 90, what is the maximum profit or loss?

    _____

24. If the futures in the previous trade move to 78, what is the maximum profit or loss?

    _____

25. Strangles are quite similar to straddles, except _____ .
    A. The options have different expiration months
    B. One option is short and the other is long
    C. The options are ITM instead of ATM
    D. The options are OTM instead of ATM

26. Long strangles involve buying both an OTM call and an OTM put with _____ .
    A. Different strike prices and identical expiration months
    B. Identical strike prices and different expiration months
    C. Identical strike prices and expiration months
    D. Different strike prices and expiration months

27. A long strangle has _____ .
    A. Limited profit potential and limited risk
    B. Limited profit potential and unlimited risk
    C. Unlimited profit potential and unlimited risk
    D. Unlimited profit potential and limited risk

28. Calculate the following values using this long strangle example:

    > Long 1 Oct Gold Futures OTM 310 Put @ 3.25
    > Long 1 Oct Gold Futures OTM 350 Call @ 2.55

    Gold is currently trading at 330.

    Put cost = _____

    Call cost = _____

    Maximum reward = _____

    Maximum risk = _____

    Upside break-even = _____

    Downside break-even = _____

    Range of profitability = _____

29. Selling a strangle involves selling both an OTM call and an OTM put with _____ .

    A. Different strike prices and identical expiration months
    B. Identical strike prices and different expiration months
    C. Identical strike prices and expiration months
    D. Different strike prices and expiration months

30. Why is the profit potential for a short strangle less than the profit potential for a short straddle?

    _____

    _____

    _____

31. Calculate the values below for the following short strangle example:

    Short 1 Jun Swiss Deutsche Mark Futures OTM 54 Put @ 9.9
    Short 1 Jun Swiss Deutsche Mark Futures OTM 60 Call @ 10.4

    Swiss deutsche mark futures are currently trading at 57.

    Put cost = _____

    Call cost = _____

    Maximum reward = _____

    Maximum risk = _____

    Upside break-even = _____

    Downside break-even = _____

    Range of profitability = _____

32. True or False: Fixed straddles can be adjusted as the market moves back and forth.

33. Name two ways of creating a long synthetic straddle using a futures contract.

_____

_____

34. Calculate the values below for the following long synthetic straddle example:

> Long 1 Nov Gold Futures @ 330
> Long 2 Nov Gold Futures 330 Puts @ 6.85

Put cost = _____

Maximum reward = _____

Maximum risk = _____

Upside break-even = _____

Downside break-even = _____

Range of profitability = _____

35. Name two ways of creating a short synthetic straddle using a futures contract.

_____

_____

36. Calculate the values below for the following short synthetic strad-
    dle example:

    >Long 1 Oct Gold Futures @ 330
    >Short 2 Oct Gold Futures 330 Calls @ 7.25

    Call cost = _____

    Maximum reward = _____

    Maximum risk = _____

    Upside break-even = _____

    Downside break-even = _____

    Range of profitability = _____

13

Advanced Delta Neutral Strategies

In this chapter, the reader is introduced to various nondirectional delta neutral strategies. Ratio spreads provide a wide profit zone, but have unlimited risk. Ratio backspreads are preferably entered as credit trades and offer limited risk with unlimited reward potential.

1. A ratio spread is a strategy in which an _____ number of option contracts of the same underlying instrument are bought and sold.

    A. Even

    B. Uneven

2. A call ratio spread involves _____ .

    A. Buying a lower strike option and selling a greater number of ITM options

    B. Buying a higher strike option and selling a greater number of ATM options

    C. Buying a lower strike option and selling a greater number of OTM options

    D. Buying a higher strike option and selling a greater number of OTM options

3. Using this ratio call spread, calculate the following values:

    Long 1 Dec T-Bond Futures 114 Call @ 1^21
    Short 2 Dec T-Bond Futures 120 Calls @ 1^04

    Net credit = _____

    Maximum reward = _____

    Maximum risk = _____

    Upside break-even = _____

    Downside break-even = _____

4. A call ratio spread should be implemented in a _____ market.

    A. Bullish

    B. Bearish

    C. Either of the above

5. A put ratio spread involves _____ .

    A. Buying a higher-strike put option and selling a greater number of OTM put options

    B. Buying a lower-strike put option and selling a greater number of OTM put options

    C. Buying a higher-strike put option and selling a greater number of ITM put options

    D. Buying a lower-strike put option and selling a greater number of ITM put options

6. Using this ratio put spread, calculate the following values:

    Long 1 Dec T-Bond Futures 114 Put @ 1^08
    Short 2 Dec T-Bond Futures 108 Puts @ ^58

    Net credit = _____

    Maximum reward = _____

    Maximum risk = _____

    Upside break-even = _____

    Downside break-even = _____

7. A put ratio spread should be implemented in a _____ market.

    A. Bullish

    B. Bearish

    C. Either of the above

8. True or False: Never attempt to place a ratio backspread in a market with low volatility.

9. A call ratio backspread involves ————————— .

   A. Selling the higher-strike call and buying a greater number of lower-strike calls

   B. Selling the lower-strike call and buying a greater number of higher-strike calls

   C. Buying the lower-strike call and selling a greater number of higher-strike calls

   D. Buying the higher-strike call and selling a greater number of lower-strike calls

10. Using this call ratio backspread, calculate the following values:

   Short 2 Dec T-Bond Futures 114 Calls @ 1^29
   Long 3 Dec T-Bond Futures 116 Calls @ ^62

   Net credit = ———————————————————————

   Maximum reward = ——————————————————————

   Maximum risk = ———————————————————————

   Upside break-even = ————————————————————

   Downside break-even = ——————————————————

   Price of underlying at maximum risk = ———————————

11. Call ratio backspreads are best implemented during periods of ————————— .

   A. High volatility in a highly volatile market that shows signs of increasing activity to the upside

   B. High volatility in a highly volatile market that shows signs of increasing activity to the downside

   C. Low volatility in a highly volatile market that shows signs of increasing activity to the upside

   D. Low volatility in a highly volatile market that shows signs of increasing activity to the downside

12. Put ratio backspreads are best implemented at periods of
    _____ .
    A. High volatility in a highly volatile market that shows signs of increasing activity to the upside
    B. High volatility in a highly volatile market that shows signs of increasing activity to the downside
    C. Low volatility in a highly volatile market that shows signs of increasing activity to the upside
    D. Low volatility in a highly volatile market that shows signs of increasing activity to the downside

13. A put ratio backspread involves _____ .
    A. Selling the higher-strike put and buying a greater number of lower-strike puts
    B. Selling the lower-strike put and buying a greater number of higher-strike puts
    C. Buying the higher-strike put and selling a greater number of lower-strike puts
    D. Buying the lower-strike put and selling a greater number of higher-strike puts

14. Using this put ratio backspread, calculate the following values:

    Short 2 Dec T-Bond Futures 114 Puts @ 1^41
    Long 4 Dec T-Bond Futures 112 Puts @ ^48

    Net credit/debit = _____

    Maximum profit = _____

    Maximum risk = _____

    Upside break-even = _____

    Downside break-even = _____

    Price of underlying asset at maximum risk = _____

14

Trading Techniques for Range-Bound Markets

This chapter explores option strategies that exploit the sideways movement and the time value of options. These options include the long butterfly, long condor, and the long iron butterfly. The reader will also be introduced to short strategies that work well in markets that are ready to break out of their usual trading range.

1. In sideways markets, option strategies are based on _____ .
   A. Gamma decay
   B. Theta decay
   C. Delta neutrality
   D. Vega neutrality

2. A sideways market is a market that _____ .
   A. Has extremely low volatility
   B. Moves erratically
   C. Stays between consistent resistance and support levels
   D. Stays at the same market volume consistently

3. Name the three parts of a butterfly strategy.

   _____

   _____

   _____

4. The body of a butterfly spread contains an option with the strike price _____ .
   A. Above the resistance level
   B. Below the support level
   C. Outside the support or resistance levels
   D. In between the support and resistance levels

5. The wings of an optimal butterfly spread are comprised of _____ .
   A. Options with the strike prices outside the trading range
   B. Options with the strike prices at both ends of the trading range
   C. Options with the strike prices close to the equilibrium level
   D. One option outside the support level and one inside the resistance level

6. A long butterfly spread consists of _____ .

    A. Going long (buying) the wings and going short (selling) the body (the middle strike options)

    B. Going long (buying) the wings and going long (buying) the body (the middle strike options)

    C. Going short (selling) the wings and going long (buying) the body (the middle strike options)

    D. Going short (selling) the wings and going short (selling) the body (the middle strike options)

7. Money is made on a long butterfly when _____ .

    A. The market closes outside of the wings

    B. The market closes in between the wings and the break-even points

8. Calculate the following values in this long butterfly trade:

    Long 1 Dec IBM 100 Call @ $7^1/_2$
    Short 2 Dec IBM 105 Calls @ 5
    Long 1 Dec IBM 110 Call @ 3

    IBM is currently trading at 105.

    Net credit/debit = _____

    Maximum reward = _____

    Maximum risk = _____

    Upside break-even = _____

    Downside break-even = _____

9. A short butterfly spread consists of _____ .
   A. Going long (buying) the wings and going short (selling) the body (the middle strike options)
   B. Going long (buying) the wings and going long (buying) the body (the middle strike options)
   C. Going short (selling) the wings and going long (buying) the body (the middle strike options)
   D. Going short (selling) the wings and going short (selling) the body (the middle strike options)

10. Calculate the following values in this short butterfly trade:

    Short 1 Dec IBM 100 Call @ 7½
    Long 2 Dec IBM 105 Calls @ 5
    Short 1 Dec IBM 110 Call @ 3

    IBM is currently trading at 105.

    Net credit/debit = _____

    Maximum reward = _____

    Maximum risk = _____

    Upside break-even = _____

    Downside break-even = _____

11. In a long condor, you need to _____ .
    A. Go long the two inner option strikes of the body and go long the wings
    B. Go long the two inner option strikes of the body and go short the wings
    C. Go short the two inner option strikes of the body and go long the wings
    D. Go short the two inner option strikes of the body and go short the wings

12. Calculate the following values for this long condor trade:

> Long 1 Nov Bond Futures 108 Call @ 2^26
> Short 1 Nov Bond Futures 110 Call @ 2^01
> Short 1 Nov Bond Futures 112 Call @ 1^18
> Long 1 Nov Bond Futures 114 Call @ 1^02

Net credit/debit = _____

Maximum reward = _____

Maximum risk = _____

Upside break-even = _____

Downside break-even = _____

13. In a short condor, you _____ .
    A. Go long the two inner option strikes of the body and go long the wings
    B. Go long the two inner option strikes of the body and go short the wings
    C. Go short the two inner option strikes of the body and go long the wings
    D. Go short the two inner option strikes of the body and go short the wings

14. Calculate the following values for this short condor trade:

> Short 1 Oct Bond Futures 106 Call @ 3^14
> Long 1 Oct Bond Futures 108 Call @ 2^18
> Long 1 Oct Bond Futures 110 Call @ 1^22
> Short 1 Oct Bond Futures 112 Call @ 1^16

Net credit/debit = _____

Maximum reward = _____

Maximum risk = _____

Upside break-even = _____

Downside break-even = _____

15. A long iron butterfly is a combination of _____ .

    A. A bear call spread and a bull put spread

    B. A bear call spread and a bull call spread

    C. A bear put spread and a bull put spread

    D. A bear put spread and a bull call spread

16. Calculate the following values using this long iron butterfly trade:

    > Long 1 Nov Bond Futures 114 Call @ 1^02
    > Short 1 Nov Bond Futures 112 Call @ 1^30
    > Short 1 Nov Bond Futures 110 Put @ 1^28
    > Long 1 Nov Bond Futures 108 Put @ 1^18

    Net credit/debit = _____

    Maximum reward = _____

    Maximum risk = _____

    Upside break-even = _____

    Downside break-even = _____

17. A short iron butterfly consists of _____ .

    A. A bear call spread and a bull put spread

    B. A bear call spread and a bull call spread

    C. A bear put spread and a bull put spread

    D. A bear put spread and a bull call spread

18. Calculate the following values using this short iron butterfly trade:

> Short 1 Nov Bond Futures 112 Call @ 1^22
> Long 1 Nov Bond Futures 110 Call @ 2^04
> Long 1 Nov Bond Futures 108 Put @ 2^00
> Short 1 Nov Bond Futures 106 Put @ 1^20

Net credit/debit = _____

Maximum reward = _____

Maximum risk = _____

Upside break-even = _____

Downside break-even = _____

15

Increasing Your Profits
with Adjustments

This chapter explores the process of adjustments. When a market makes a move, it changes the overall position delta of the trade. By making an adjustment, a trader can increase profits on the trade by bringing the trade back to delta neutral.

1. Name three things you can do when the market moves and your trade is no longer delta neutral.

   _____

   _____

   _____

2. An adjustment can be made by _____ to offset your position to bring it back to delta neutral.
   A. Buying or selling options
   B. Buying or selling futures
   C. Buying or selling stocks
   D. All of the above

3. The two sides of a delta neutral trade are _____ and _____ .

4. A futures contract has a _____ delta.
   A. Fixed
   B. Variable
   C. Fixed or variable

5. Options have _____ deltas.
   A. Fixed
   B. Variable
   C. Fixed or variable

6. ATM options are easy to work with because they have _____ .
   A. Low liquidity and thin price spreads
   B. Low liquidity and large price spreads
   C. High liquidity and thin price spreads
   D. High liquidity and large price spreads

16

Processing Your Trade

Trades are executed on exchanges. This chapter explores the process that a trade goes through from beginning to end. Stocks, futures, and options trades are investigated in depth so that the reader can understand the extraordinary process a trade goes through as it is executed.

1. What are the three primary U.S. stock exchanges?

_____

_____

_____

2. U.S. exchanges are regulated by the _____ .
   A. U.S. Congress
   B. National Stock Exchange Commission
   C. Securities and Exchange Commission
   D. Securities Exchange Act

3. _____ is an illegal form of trading in which corporate officers buy and sell stock in their company prior to important information being released.
   A. Corporate raiding
   B. Security trading
   C. Market trading
   D. Insider trading

4. The _____ regulates the nation's commodity futures exchanges.
   A. Commodities Futures Trading Commission
   B. Security and Exchange Commission
   C. National Commodity Exchange Commission
   D. U.S. Congress

5. Describe the process your order goes through to get filled at a stock exchange.

_____

_____

_____

6. _____ at exchanges create liquidity and narrow the spreads.
   A. Specialists
   B. Floor brokers
   C. Market makers
   D. Exchange officers

7. Orders are filled by a system of _____ at a commodities exchange.
   A. Electronic review
   B. Specialist making transaction matches
   C. Market makers "making" a market
   D. Open outcry

8. Floor traders make most of their money on _____ .
   A. Bid/ask spread
   B. Commissions
   C. Leasing their seats
   D. All of the above

9. The _____ is the highest-volume stock options exchange.
   A. New York Stock Exchange (NYSE)
   B. Chicago Board Options Exchange (CBOE)
   C. American Stock Exchange (AMEX)
   D. Pacific Stock Exchange (PSE)

17

Placing Orders

It is essential to master the art of placing orders. This chapter investigates how to find a good broker as well as the order process itself. Examples are include to guide the reader through this precise process.

1. A _____ is an individual who is licensed to buy and sell marketplace securities and/or derivatives directly to traders and investors.
   A. Market maker
   B. Speculator
   C. Arbitrageur
   D. Broker

2. True or False: If someone is licensed to take an order, that person must have the knowledge to invest your money wisely.

3. Your broker, as your intermediary, will get paid a _____ for each transaction.
   A. Round turn
   B. Arbitrage
   C. Commission
   D. Dividend

4. True or False: After your broker has made a suggestion, never make an investment while still on the phone. Put the phone down. Think about what was told to you and do your analysis of risk and reward.

5. Placing _____ initiates a process in which you execute a trade.
   A. An order
   B. A spread
   C. A fill or kill
   D. A stop

6. A _____ is the price you are given on an executed trade.
   A. Buy
   B. Bid
   C. Ask
   D. Fill

7. Make a list of important items that need to be specified when placing an order.

   _____

   _____

   _____

   _____

   _____

   _____

   _____

8. If you place a _____ , you will get an immediate fill
   at the current price.
   A. Limit order
   B. Market order
   C. Day order
   D. Stop order

9. If you place a _____ , you have to wait until the
   price you want gets hit before the broker can execute your trade.
   A. Limit order
   B. Market order
   C. Day order
   D. Stop order

10. If you want to place a market order to sell one September S&P 500
    futures contract and buy two September S&P 500 Futures 940 ATM
    calls, what would you tell your broker?

    _____

    _____

    _____

11. If you are doing a ratio backspread—buying 10 S&P 500 Futures 935 puts and selling 5 September S&P 500 Futures 940 puts with 15.35 to the buy side and 12.75 to the sell side—what would the point difference be?

_____

12. The more volatile the market is, the _____ the bid/ask spread will be.
    A. Narrower
    B. Wider
    C. More consistent
    D. More fluctuating

13. Floor prices primarily depend on _____ .
    A. Your broker's execution and the exchange
    B. Bid/ask spread and volatility
    C. Bid/ask spread and liquidity
    D. Liquidity and volatility

Appendix

Trading Media Sources

1. The *Wall Street Journal* is one of the best newspapers a trader can use to spot good investment opportunities. Match the sections below with the correct definition.

What's News

1. The column represents those stocks with the highest trading records.

Money & Investing

2. This column reveals the number of shares of stock traded per day which is important when the volume is increasing significantly.

Most Active Issues

3. This column shows the number of contracts or units being held in a futures market. It is of limited use because a great majority of the trading and open interest contracts are created by hedging practices primarily generated by large commercial traders and speculators.

Price Percentage Gainers . . . and Losers

4. This column can be used effectively to scan for news that is dramatically bullish or bearish; then you watch the stocks to see how they react once the information is in the marketplace.

Volume Percentage Leaders

5. For options, the months corresponding to the expiration of the options that were bought or sold. This information is vital to determining the available contracts which can be traded and to develop profit-making strategies.

Marketplace	6. The first page contains a series of five charts and graphs—stocks, bonds, interest, U.S. dollar, and commodities. The second page contains a wide variety of important trading graphs and percentages.
Stock Page Headings	7. These columns represent yesterday's high price and low price for futures contracts. This has much more meaning than in stock trading, as the futures traders are more short-term–oriented.
52 Weeks Hi and Lo	8. This column shows the price-to-earnings ratio, which is very important because it tells you how many times the earnings a stock is trading at.
Yld and %	9. This column details the high and low price as of yesterday. Investors and traders look at this information to signal if stock traders will be running stops.
PE	10. This column establishes the starting point for where a futures contract traded when the market opened.
Vol	11. First read of the day. In just a few minutes, this section summarizes the most important information you need.
Hi/Lo	12. This column reveals a futures market's highest and lowest prices since inception, which translate to very strong resistance (for highs) and support (for lows) levels.
Close/Net Chg	13. For options, this column shows the price at which the underlying asset is sold or bought if exercised, which is used to determine the available contracts that can be traded and to develop profit-making strategies.
Open	14. This column shows the dividend yield (the return you make on a dividend payout) and earnings of a particular stock.
High/Low	15. These two figures show the closing price and the change in price yesterday, which signals the dollar value a stock has changed.
Settle	16. This figure tells you the price change of a stock over the last year. The difference between the high and low is called the range.
Lifetime High and Low	17. A list of stocks showing the highest-volume trading. Although many of the same stocks show up here day after day, you want to locate those that are new to the list to find profitable trade opportunities.

Open Interest   18. This column reflects how much yesterday's closing
                           price changed compared to the previous day's close
                           for futures.

Strike Price   19. A major section that contains a variety of important
                           and not-so-important stock analyses.

Expiration Months   20. Two columns that reveal the stocks with the greatest
                           up or down momentum.

PART TWO

Answers

1

Introduction to Options Trading

1. True
2. An investor takes a long-term, relatively passive approach. A trader takes an active approach using strategies to capitalize on shorter-term market movement.
3. B—Funds
4. D—Time constraints
5. D—All of the above
6. C—Defining your risk in every trade
7. A—Flexibility
8. A—Specialize
9. B—Patience and persistence

2

The Big Picture

---

1. The total number of outstanding shares, the value of the equity of the company (what it owns less what it owes), the earnings the company produces now and is expected to produce in the future, and the demand for the shares of the company.

2. B—$12,500

3. C—NASDAQ

4. C—Liquidity

5. C—Be bid up

6. D—Decline

7. Rise. Fall.

8. D—Dividend

9. Blue chips, mid caps, small caps

10. D—Dow Jones Industrial Average

11. Technologies, defense, retail, health, financial, consumer products

12. A futures contract is a promise to actually make a transaction, whereas an option is the right, but not the obligation, to buy or sell an underlying instrument (unless you are the option seller).

13. B—Futures contracts

14. C—Hedgers
15. B—Speculators
16. A—Go long
17. B—Go short
18. Physical. Financial.
19. Agricultural products, foods, meats, metals, energies
20. D—All of the above
21. A—The U.S. dollar
22. C—An index
23. D—All of the above
24. C—Options
25. A—Premium
26. B—Strike price
27. B—Expiration date
28. False. Options are not always available on every stock or futures contract.
29. B—100
30. True. You are responsible for understanding the specifications for each futures market.
31. B—$250 (e.g., the S&P 500)
32. B—Liquidity
33. D—Liquidity and volatility
34. D—Liquidity
35. A —Volatility

3

Elements of a Good Investment

---

1. Low risk, favorable risk profile, high potential return, meets your time constraints, meets your risk tolerance level, can be easily understood, meets your investment criteria, meets your investment capital constraints

2. B—The risk/reward profile

3. C—Price

4. A—High reward

5. False

6. D—Available investment capital

7. Capital gains, interest income, security

4

A Short Course in Investment Economics

1. D—30-year T-bond
2. B—Down
3. A—Go in the same direction
4. A—Rise
5. C—A divergence
6. A—Increasing
7. D—Stable or decreasing

5

How to Spot Explosive Opportunities

1. Fundamental analysis, technical analysis

2. A—Fundamental

3. Products, customers, consumption, profit outlook, management strength, supply of and demand for outputs, economic data

4. B—Technical

5. Moving average, momentum indicator

6. B—Moving average

7. C—Momentum indicator

8. D—Contrarian

9. False

10. D—All of the above

11. Find out what products are "hot."
    Notice which products have the most store shelf exposure.
    Ask a clerk which products are literally flying off the shelf.

12. Take notice of companies and franchises where you get a good deal as to price, quality, and quantity.
    Critique that which you already own.
    Ask your children what's hot and what's not.
    Look around where you work for popular products and services.

13. Real time, delayed, end-of-day

14. False

15. B—CNBC

16. C—Momentum

17. B—Volume

18. C—P/E

19. Stocks with greatest percentage rise in volume
    Stocks with an increase in price greater than 30 percent
    Stocks with a decrease in price greater than 30 percent
    Stocks with strong (buying) or weak (selling) EPS growth
    Stocks with strong (buying) or weak (selling) relative strength
    Stocks making a new 52-week high or new 52-week low

20. Wayne Huzienga

21. B—$20

22. D—All of the above

23. C—Both A and B

24. A—Short-term

25. F—Both C and D (60 and 90 days)

26. D—30 percent

27. A—Price and volume

28. B—300,000

29. B—Price percentage losers

30. C—Low price

6

Option Basics

---

1. B—An option

2. D—Premium

3. False. Options are not available on every stock or futures contract.

4. False. You are not obligated to buy or sell the underlying instrument. You can simply let the option expire worthless.

5. C—Expires

6. A—Debit

7. B—Credit

8. D—Strike prices

9. A—Expensive

10. True

11. In-the-money (ITM), at-the-money (ATM), out-of-the-money (OTM)

12. American-style options can be exercised at any time on or before their expiration dates. European-style options can be exercised only on (not before) their expiration dates.

13. The option may expire and become worthless, be exercised by its owner, or be assigned.

14. C—An exercise notice

15. B—100

16. C—Third

17. C—$5

18. True

19. Calls, puts

20. A—A call option

21. B—In-the-money

22. C—Out-of-the-money

23. A—At-the-money

24. A—Going long

25. B—Going short

26. B—Bullish

27. A—Bearish

28. D—The price of the premium and brokerage commissions

29. A—Unlimited

30. | *Strike Price of Option* | *Call Option* |
| --- | --- |
| 320 | OTM |
| 315 | OTM |
| 310 | OTM |
| 305 | OTM |
| 300 | ATM |
| 295 | ITM |
| 290 | ITM |
| 285 | ITM |
| 280 | ITM |

31. If the underlying asset increases in price before the option expires, the holder can purchase the underlying asset for the lower strike price.

If the underlying asset's price increases before expiration, the value of the option increases and the option can be sold at a profit.

32. B—An option series

33. B—A put option

34. B—In-the-money

35. C—Out-of-the-money

36. A—At-the-money

37. B—Going short

38. A—Going long

39. A—Bearish

40. B—Bullish

41. D—The price of the premium and brokerage commissions

42. A—Unlimited

43.

Strike Price of Option	*Put Option*
320	ITM
315	ITM
310	ITM
305	ITM
300	ATM
295	OTM
290	OTM
285	OTM
280	OTM

7

Introduction to Delta Neutral Trading

1. E—Both A & B (High liquidity and high volatility, high liquidity and low volatility)

2. True

3. D—Liquidity

4. False. Delta neutral strategies are best used for longer-term trades.

5. A—Dividing the change in the premium by the change in the price of the underlying asset

6. D—Plus or minus 100

7. A—Positive

8. A—Positive

9. A—In-the-money

10. C—At-the-money

11. A—In-the-money

12. D—Plus 200

8

The Greeks and Option Pricing

1. C—Risk exposures

2. Delta, gamma, theta, vega, zeta.

3. | *Greek* | *Definition* |
   |---|---|
   | Gamma | Change in the delta of an option with respect to the change in price of its underlying security |
   | Zeta | The percentage change in an option's price per 1 percent change in implied volatility |
   | Delta | Change in the price of an option relative to the price change of the underlying security |
   | Theta | Change in the price of an option with respect to a change in its time to expiration |
   | Vega | Change in the price of an option with respect to its change in volatility |

4. A—Intrinsic value and extrinsic value

5. B—In-the-money

6. C—The current price of the underlying asset minus the strike price of the call option

7. A—The strike price of the put option minus the current price of the underlying asset

8. D—Zero

9. D—Zero

10. True

11. B—Decreases

12. C—Theta

13. D—All of the above

14.

Price of Gold = 300

Call Strike Price	January	March	Intrinsic Value	Time Value Jan	Time Value Mar
295	12.5	15.75	5	7.5	10.75
300	5	8.5	0	5	8.5
305	1.5	3.75	0	1.5	3.75

15. C—Out-of-the-money

16. C—Intrinsic value

17. A—In-the-money

18. The current price of the underlying financial instrument
The strike price of the option
The type of option (put or call)
The amount of time remaining until expiration
The current risk-free interest rate
The dividend rate, if any, of the underlying financial instrument
The volatility of the underlying financial instrument

19. D—Volatility

20. Implied volatility approximates how much the marketplace thinks prices will move and is calculated by using an option pricing model (Black-Scholes for stocks and indexes and Black for futures).

Historical volatility gauges price movement in terms of past performance and is calculated by using the standard deviation of underlying asset price changes from close to close of trading going back 21 to 23 days (or any predetermined time frame).

21. Understanding volatility helps in choosing and implementing the appropriate option strategy, holds the key to improving market timing, and helps avoid the purchase of overpriced options and the sale of underpriced options.

22. D—Vega

23. A—Up

24. B—First Friday

25. B—Drops

26. C—Buying options with low volatility and selling options with high volatility

9

Risk Profiles

---

1. D—All of the above
2. A—Market price of the underlying asset
3. C—Profit and loss
4. Figure 1—Short put; Figure 2—Short futures or stock; Figure 3—Long put; Figure 4—Short call; Figure 5—Long futures or stock; Figure 6—Long call
5. C—Unlimited profit potential with unlimited risk (down to zero)
6. A—1 to 1
7. True
8. C—Unlimited profit potential (to an asset price of zero) with unlimited risk
9. True
10. D—Unlimited profit potential with limited risk
11. False. Zero margin borrowing is allowed, which means that you don't have to hold any margin in your account to place the trade.
12. C—$500 plus commissions
13. A—Adding the cost of the option to its strike price
14. False. In a short call strategy, when the underlying instrument's price falls, you make money; when it rises, you lose money.

15. B—Limited profit potential with unlimited risk

16. True

17. D—Unlimited profit potential with limited risk

18. D—Subtracting the option premium from the strike price

19. False. In a short put strategy, when the underlying instrument's price rises, you make money; when it falls, you lose money.

20. B—Limited profit potential and unlimited risk (until the asset reaches zero)

10

Risk and Margin

---

1. Limited risk, unlimited reward
2. The size of the transaction (number of shares/futures or options) and the risk calculated on the trade
3. B—Cash trade
4. A—Margin trade
5. D—Margin
6. B—Margin account
7. B—50 percent
8. C—$25,000. The brokerage firm loans you the other half for a total of $50,000.
9. D—Margin call
10. False. If your futures side starts losing money, you will be required to post margin for the option side.
11. D—Perceived risk
12. B—Liquidated
13. C—50 percent
14. B—$100

15. A—Naked
16. B—Decrease
17. C—Commodities
18. D—Leverage

11

Basic Trading Strategies

---

1. Strategic trades, long-term trades, delta neutral trades
2. False. Strategic trades are geared for traders who do have the time to monitor the markets closely each day.
3. True
4. E—Zero
5. C—Buying or selling trading instruments
6. A—Covered write
7. B—Decrease in price
8. B—Limited profit potential with unlimited risk
9. D—Bull call spread
10. A—Limited profit potential with limited risk
11. Maximum risk = net debit = 7.80 – 4.25 = 3.55 × $100 = $355

    Maximum reward = difference between strike prices less debit = 330 – 310 = 20 × $100 = $2000 – $355 = $1645

    Break-even = Lower strike price plus the net debit = 310 + 3.55 = 313.55
12. E—Bull put spread

13. A—Limited profit potential with limited risk

14. Maximum risk = difference in strike prices times value per point, less net credit = $(330 - 320) \times \$100 - \$375 = \$625$

    Maximum reward = net credit = $10.50 - 6.75 = 3.75 \times \$100 = \$375$

    Break-even = higher strike price minus net credit = $330 - 3.75 = 326.25$

15. B—Bear call spread

16. A—Limited profit potential with limited risk

17. Maximum risk = difference in strike times value per point, less net credit = $(90 - 80) \times \$100 - \$450 = \$550$

    Maximum reward = net credit = $11.50 - 7.00 = 4.50 \times \$100 = \$450$

    Break-even = lower strike call plus net credit = $80 + 4.50 = 84.50$

18. C—Bear put spread

19. A—Limited profit potential with limited risk

20. Maximum risk = net debit = $3\frac{3}{4} - 2\frac{1}{2} = 1\frac{1}{4} \times \$100 = \$125$

    Maximum reward = difference in strike prices times value per point, minus net debit = $(95 - 90) \times \$100 - \$125 = \$375$

    Break-even = higher strike less net debit = $95 - 1\frac{1}{4} = 93\frac{3}{4}$

12

The Nuts and Bolts of Delta Neutral Trading

1. D—Zero
2. B—100
3. False. One hundred shares of any stock or one futures contract equals plus or minus 100 deltas.
4. C—Strike price
5. B—Bullish
6. A—Bearish
7. Buy two ATM puts. Sell two ATM calls.
8. Buy two ATM calls. Sell two ATM puts.
9. D—Unlimited profit potential with limited risk
10. B—Limited profit potential with unlimited risk
11. A—U-shaped risk curve with unlimited profit potential and limited risk
12. D—Upside-down U-shaped risk curve with limited profit potential and unlimited risk
13. C—Identical strike prices and expiration months

14. B—Low volatility expecting a volatility increase

15. A—U-shaped risk curves with unlimited profit potential and limited risk

16. Upside break-even = strike price plus net premium debit

17. Downside break-even = strike price less net premium debit

18. Put cost = 5.55 × $100 = $555

    Call cost = 7.20 × $100 = $720

    Maximum reward = unlimited to the upside or downside

    Maximum risk = net debit paid = 5.55 + 7.20 = 12.75 × $100 = $1275

    Upside break-even = strike price plus net debit = 330 + 12.75 = 342.75

    Downside break-even = strike price minus net debit = 330 – 12.75 = 317.25

    Range of profitability = unlimited beyond break-even points

19. C—Identical strike prices and expiration months

20. A—High volatility (and expect a decrease in volatility)

21. D—Upside-down U-shaped risk curves with limited profit potential and unlimited risk

22. Maximum put profit = 2.22 × $1250 = $2775

    Maximum call profit = 3.24 × $1250 = $4050

    Maximum reward = net credit = $2775 + $4050 = $6825

    Maximum risk = unlimited to the upside or downside

    Upside break-even = strike price plus net debit = 84 + 5.46 = 89.46

    Downside break-even = strike price minus net debit = 84 – 5.46 = 78.54

    Range of profitability = 89.46 to 78.54

23. $675 loss: (90 – 89.46) × value per point = .54 × $1250 = $675

24. $675 loss: [(84 − 78) − 5.46] × $1250 = $675

25. D—The options are OTM instead of ATM

26. A—Different strike prices and identical expiration months

27. D—Unlimited profit potential and limited risk

28. Put cost = 3.25 × $100 = $325

    Call cost = 2.55 × $100 = $255

    Maximum reward = unlimited to the upside or downside

    Maximum risk = net debit = $255 + $325 = $580

    Upside break-even = Call strike plus net debit = 350 + 5.80 = 355.80

    Downside break-even = put strike minus net debit = 310 − 5.80 = 304.20

    Range of profitability = unlimited beyond break-even points

29. A—Different strike prices and identical expiration months

30. The profit potential for a short strangle is less than the profit potential for a short straddle because a short strangle involves selling OTM options instead of ATM options, and OTM options have smaller premiums and therefore deliver a reduced overall credit to the seller.

31. Put cost = (.99 × $1250) = $1237.50

    Call cost = (1.04 × $1250) = $1300

    Maximum reward = net credit = $1237.50 + $1300 = $2537.50

    Maximum risk = unlimited to the upside or downside

    Upside break-even = call strike plus net credit = 60 + 2.03 = 62.03

    Downside break-even = put strike minus net credit = 54 − 2.03 = 51.97

    Range of profitability = 51.97 to 62.03

32. False. Fixed straddles cannot be adjusted.

33. Sell one futures and buy two ATM calls.
    Buy one futures and buy two ATM puts.

34. Put Cost = $(6.85 \times 2) \times 100 = \$1370$.

    Maximum reward = unlimited

    Maximum risk = net debit = $6.85 \times 2 = 13.70 \times \$100 = \$1370$

    Upside break-even = price of underlying at initiation plus net debit = $330 + 13.70 = 343.70$

    Downside break-even = price of underlying at initiation minus net debit = $330 - 3.7 = 316.30$

    Range of profitability = unlimited beyond break-even points

35. Buy one futures and sell two ATM calls.

    Sell one futures and sell two ATM puts.

36. Call Cost = $(7.25 \times 2) \times 100 = \$1450$ credit.

    Maximum profit = net credit = $7.25 \times 2 = 14.5 \times \$100 = \$1450$

    Maximum risk = unlimited

    Upside break-even = price of underlying at initiation plus net credit = $330 + 14.50 = 344.50$

    Downside break-even = price of underlying at initiation minus net credit = $330 - 14.50 = 315.50$

    Range of profitability = limited between the break-even points of 315.5 and 344.5

13

Advanced Delta Neutral Strategies

---

1. B—Uneven

2. C—Buying a lower strike option and selling a greater number of OTM options

3. Net credit $= 2 \times [(1 \times \$1000) + (4 \times 15.625)] - [(1 \times \$1000) + (21 \times 15.625)] = \$2125 - \$1328 = \$797 = {}^{51}/_{64}$

   Maximum reward = (difference in strikes times value per point) plus net credit $= [(120 - 114) \times \$1000 + \$797 = \$6797]$ (when underlying hits higher strike)

   Maximum risk = unlimited to the upside above upside break-even point

   Upside break-even = lower strike call price plus {[(difference in strike prices) × number of short contracts] ÷ (number of short contracts minus number of long contracts)} plus net credit received $= 114 + \{[(120 - 114) \times 2] \div (2 - 1)\} + {}^{51}/_{64} = 114 + 12 + {}^{51}/_{64} = 126{}^{51}/_{64} = 126{}^{25.5}/_{32}$

   Downside break-even = none (credit trade)

4. B—Bearish

5. A—Buying a higher-strike put option and selling a greater number of OTM put options

6. Net credit = $[2 \times (58 \times 15.625)] - [(1 \times \$1000) + (8 \times 15.625)] = \$1812.50 - \$1125 = \$687.50$

Maximum profit = (difference in strikes × value per point) plus net credit = $[(114 - 108) \times \$1000) + \$687.50] = \$6687.50$ (when underlying hits lower strike)

Maximum risk = unlimited to the downside below the break-even point

Upside break-even = none (done at a credit)

Downside break-even = higher put strike price minus {[(difference in strikes) times the number of short contracts] divided by (number of short contracts minus long contracts)} minus the net credit received = $114 - \{[(114 - 108) \times 2] \div (2 - 1)\} - {}^{44}/_{64} = 114 - (12 \div 1) - {}^{44}/_{64} = 102 - {}^{44}/_{64} = 101 {}^{20}/_{64} + 101 {}^{10}/_{32}$

7. A—Bullish

8. False. Placing ratio backspreads in markets with low volatility is not recommended; however, if you do choose to trade a slow market, follow these three rules: (1) use a .75 ratio or higher; (2) buy the lower strike; (3) sell the higher strike.

9. B—Selling the lower-strike call and buying a greater number of higher-strike calls

10. Net credit = $2 \times [(1 \times \$1000) + (29 \times 15.625)] - [3 \times (62 \times 15.625)] = \$2906 - \$2906 = 0$

Maximum profit = unlimited to the upside

Maximum risk = [(number of short calls times difference in strikes) times value per point] minus net credit = $[(2 \times 2) \times \$1000] - 0 = \$4000$

Upside break-even = higher call strike price plus {[(difference in strikes) times (number of short calls)] divided by (number of long calls minus short calls)} minus net credit received = $116 + \{[(116 - 114) \times 2] \div (3 - 2)\} - 0 = 116 + [4 \div 1] - 0 = 120$

Downside break-even = strike price of short options plus net credit = $(114 + 0) = 114$.

Price of underlying at maximum risk = 116 (long strike price)

11. C—Low volatility in a highly volatile market that shows signs of increasing activity to the upside

12. D—Low volatility in a highly volatile market that shows signs of increasing activity to the downside

13. A—Selling the higher-strike put and buying a greater number of lower-strike puts

14. Net credit = $[2 \times (1 \times \$1000) + (^{41}/_{64} \times \$1000)] - [4 \times (^{48}/_{64} \times \$1000)] = \$3281 - \$3000 = \$281 = {}^{18}/_{64}$

    Maximum profit = unlimited to the downside

    Maximum risk = [(number of short puts times difference in strikes) times value per point] minus net credit = $\{[2 \times (114 - 112) \times 1000]\} - 281 = 4000 - 281 = \$3719$

    Upside break-even = higher strike put option minus net credit = $114 - {}^{18}/_{64} = 113^{46}/_{64} = 113^{23}/_{32}$

    Downside break-even = lower strike price minus [(number of short puts times difference in strikes) divided by (number of long puts minus number of short puts) plus the net credit] = $112 - [(2 \times 2) / (4 - 2)] + {}^{18}/_{64} = (112 - 2) + {}^{18}/_{64} = 110^{18}/_{64} = 110^{9}/_{32}$

    Price of underlying asset at maximum risk = 112 (long strike price)

14

Trading Techniques for Range-Bound Markets

---

1. B—Theta decay
2. C—Stays between consistent resistance and support levels
3. The body; wing #1; wing #2
4. D—In between the support and resistance levels
5. B—Options with the strike prices at both ends of the trading range
6. A—Going long (buying) the wings and going short (selling) the body (the middle strike options)
7. B—The market closes in between the wings and the break-even points
8. Net debit = $[(7\frac{1}{2} \times \$100) + (3 \times \$100)] - (2 \times 5 \times \$100) = -\$50$

   Maximum reward = difference in strikes times value per point, less debit paid = $\$450 \ [(5 \times \$100) - \$50]$

   Maximum risk = limited to the net debit paid= $- \$50$

   Upside break-even = higher strike less net debit = $(110 - \frac{1}{2}) = 109\frac{1}{2}$

   Downside break-even = lower strike plus net debit = $(100 + \frac{1}{2}) = 100\frac{1}{2}$

9. C—Going short (selling) the wings and going long (buying) the body (the middle strike options)

10. Net credit = $[(7^1/_2 \times \$100) + (3 \times \$100)] - (5 \times 2 \times \$100) = \$50$

    Maximum reward = net credit = $50

    Maximum risk = difference in middle and lower strikes times value per point, less net credit = $[(105 - 100) \times \$100] - \$50 = \$450$

    Upside break-even = higher strike less net credit = $110 - ^1/_2 = 109^1/_2$

    Downside break-even = lower strike plus net credit = $100 + ^1/_2 = 100^1/_2$

11. C—Go short the two inner option strikes of the body and go long the wings

12. Net credit/debit = $[(2^26 + 1^02) - (2^01 + 1^18)] = 3^28 - 3^19 = ^09 = \$140.62$ debit

    Maximum reward = difference in higher and lower strikes times value per point, less net debit = $[(114 - 112) \times \$1000] - 140.62 = \$2000 - 140.62 = \$1859.38$

    Maximum risk = net debit = $140.62

    Upside break-even = higher strike minus net debit = $114 - ^09 = 113^{55}/_{64} = 113^{27.5}/_{32}$

    Downside break-even = Lower strike plus net debit = $108 + ^09 = 108^9/_{64} = 108^{4.5}/_{32}$

13. B—Go long the two inner option strikes of the body and go short the wings

14. Net credit = $[(3^14 + 1^16) - (2^18 + 1^22)] = 4^30 - 3^40 = ^54 = \$843.75$

    Maximum profit = net credit = $843.75

    Maximum risk = difference between lowest and next higher strike times value per point, less net credit = $[(108 - 106 \times 1000] - 843.75 = \$1156.25$

    Upside break-even = higher short strike less net credit = $112 - ^54 = 111^{10}/_{64} = 111^05$ (futures)

    Downside break-even = lower short strike plus net credit = $106 + ^54 = 106^{54}/_{64} = 106^{27}/_{32}$

15. A—A bear call spread and a bull put spread

16. Net credit = [(1^30 + 1^28) − (1^02 + 1^18)] = 2^58 − 2^20 = ^38 = \$593.75

    Maximum reward = net credit = \$593.75

    Maximum risk = difference in long and short strikes times value per point, less net credit = [(114 − 112) × \$1000] − 593.75 = \$2000 − 593.75 = \$1406.25

    Upside break-even = lower call strike price plus net credit = 112 + ^38 = 112$^{38}/_{64}$ = 112$^{19}/_{32}$

    Downside break-even = higher put strike price minus net credit = 110 − ^38 = 109$^{26}/_{64}$ = 109$^{13}/_{32}$

17. D—A bear put spread and a bull call spread

18. Net credit/debit = [(2^04 + 2^00) − (1^22 + 1^20)] = 4^04 − 2^42 = 1^26 = \$1406.25 debit

    Maximum reward = difference between long and short strikes times value per point, less debit paid = [(108 − 106) × \$1000] × 1406.25 = \$593.75

    Maximum risk = net debit = \$1406.25

    Upside break-even = higher long strike plus net debit = 110 + 1^26 = 111$^{26}/_{64}$ = 111^13 (futures)

    Downside break-even = lower long strike less net debit = 108 − 1^26 = 106$^{38}/_{64}$ = 106^19 (futures)

15

Increasing Your Profits with Adjustments

1. Exit the trade; maintain the trade as is; make an adjustment
2. D—All of the above
3. A—Hedge; directional bet
4. A—Fixed
5. B—Variable
6. C—High liquidity and thin price spreads

16

Processing Your Trade

1. New York Stock Exchange (NYSE), American Stock Exchange (AMEX), National Association of Securities Dealers Automated Quotations (NASDAQ)

2. C—Securities and Exchange Commission

3. D—Insider trading

4. A—Commodities Futures Trading Commission

5. You call your broker who passes your order along via DOT or by wire to a floor broker. The floor broker tries to immediately fill your order or takes it directly to a specialist who matches your order. You then receive a call from your broker with confirmation that your order has been executed.

6. C—Market makers

7. D—Open outcry

8. A—Bid/ask spread

9. B—Chicago Board Options Exchange (CBOE)

17

Placing Orders

---

1. D—Broker
2. False
3. C—Commission
4. True
5. A—An order
6. D—Fill
7. What kind of order you wish to place

    The exchange—where the order is to be placed (for futures and options)

    Quantity—number of contracts

    Buy/sell—puts or calls (also include the strike price and expiration)

    Contract—name of the contract

    Month—delivery month of the contract

    Price—instructions regarding price execution (debit or credit for stock or buy side or sell side for futures)
8. B—Market order
9. A—Limit order

10. I want to buy two September/Labor Day S&P 500 Futures 940 calls at (fill in price) and sell one September/Labor Day S&P futures at the market.

11. A 10.15 debit to the buy side [(2 × 12.75) − 15.35 = 10.15].

12. B—Wider

13. D—Liquidity and volatility

Appendix

Trading Media Sources

What's News	11. First read of the day. In just a few minutes, this section summarizes the most important information you need.
Money & Investing	6. The first page contains a series of five charts and graphs—stocks, bonds, interest, U.S. dollar, and commodities. The second page contains a wide variety of important trading graphs and percentages.
Most Active Issues	17. A list of stocks showing the highest-volume trading. Although many of the same stocks show up here day after day, you want to locate those that are new to the list to find profitable trade opportunities.
Price Percentage Gainers . . . and Losers	20. Two columns that reveal the stocks with the greatest up or down momentum.
Volume Percentage Leaders	1. The column represents those stocks with the highest trading records.
Marketplace	4. This column can be used effectively to scan for news that is dramatically bullish or bearish; then you watch the stocks to see how they react once the information is in the marketplace.
Stock Page Headings	19. A major section that contains a variety of important and not-so-important stock analyses.

52 Weeks Hi and Lo	16. This figure tells you the price change of a stock over the last year. The difference between the high and low is called the range.
Yld and %	14. This column shows the dividend yield (the return you make on a dividend payout) and earnings of a particular stock.
PE	8. This column shows the price-to-earnings ratio, which is very important because it tells you how many times the earnings a stock is trading at.
Vol	2. This column reveals the number of shares of stock traded per day which is important when the volume is increasing significantly.
Hi/Lo	9. This column details the high and low price as of yesterday. Investors and traders look at this information to signal if stock traders will be running stops.
Close/Net Chg	15. These two figures show the closing price and the change in price yesterday, which signals the dollar value a stock has changed.
Open	10. This column establishes the starting point for where a futures contract traded when the market opened.
High/Low	7. These columns represent yesterday's high price and low price for futures contracts. This has much more meaning than in stock trading, as the futures traders are more short-term–oriented.
Settle	18. This column reflects how much yesterday's closing price changed compared to the previous day's close for futures.
Lifetime High and Low	12. This column reveals a futures market's highest and lowest prices since inception, which translate to very strong resistance (for highs) and support (for lows) levels.
Open Interest	3. This column shows the number of contracts or units being held in a futures market. It is of limited use because a great majority of the trading and open interest contracts are created by hedging practices primarily generated by large commercial traders and speculators.

Strike Price   13. For options, this column shows the price at which
                         the underlying asset is sold or bought if exercised,
                         which is used to determine the available contracts
                         that can be traded and to develop profit-making
                         strategies.

Expiration Months   5. For options, the months corresponding to the expi-
                         ration of the options that were bought or sold. This
                         information is vital to determining the available con-
                         tracts which can be traded and to develop profit-
                         making strategies.

23
YEARS
ON
FIRE